MY FIRST
UKULELE

Ben Parker

Learn To Play
Right Away!

Author: Ben Parker

Edited by: Alison McNicol

First published in 2012 by Kyle Craig Publishing

This version updated Dec 2014

Text and illustration copyright © 2012 Kyle Craig Publishing

Design and illustration: Julie Anson

Music set by Ben Parker using Sibelius software

ISBN: 978-1-908707-11-6

A CIP record for this book is available from the British Library.

A Kyle Craig Publication
www.kyle-craig.com

Contents

Welcome To Your 'My First Ukulele Book'!

The ukulele is a great instrument to learn and play, and because it only has four strings, it is nice and easy to master, and you can learn quickly…with the help of this book you could be strumming and singing along to your ukulele in no time.

The book is full of well-known songs, and lots of funny limericks and rhymes, so you can have lots of fun entertaining your friends and family as you learn!

Like any new skill, it will take a little while before you get the hang of things. The more that you practice playing your uke, the easier it will become and the better you will be.

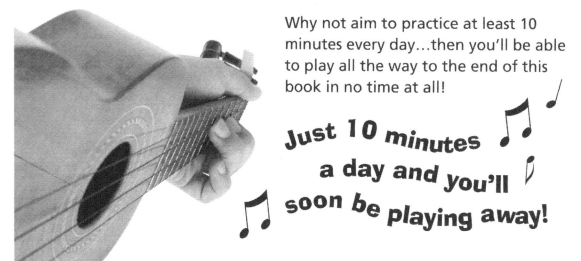

Why not aim to practice at least 10 minutes every day…then you'll be able to play all the way to the end of this book in no time at all!

Just 10 minutes a day and you'll soon be playing away!

About The Ukulele

The ukulele originates from Hawaii and is an adaptation of string instruments brought to the island by Portuguese immigrants in the late 1800's. It comes in four different sizes: **soprano**, **concert**, **tenor** and **baritone**. The most common beginners instrument is the smallest — the **soprano** ukulele.

The Parts Of A Ukulele

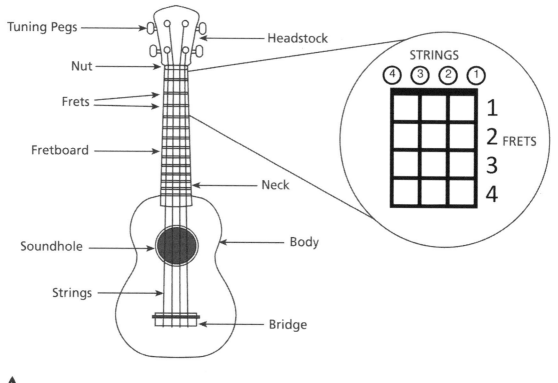

Tuning Pegs

Headstock

Nut

Frets

Fretboard

Neck

Soundhole

Body

Strings

Bridge

STRINGS

④ ③ ② ①

1
2 FRETS
3
4

How To Hold Your Ukulele

You can play the ukulele whilst standing up or sitting down. Your right arm should be able to hold it in place by pulling it into your body. At first, you may find it easier to play sitting down.

What To Do With Your Hands

LEFT HAND POSITION

Your left hand position is really important. Make sure your thumb is around the back of the neck. When you fret a note it should be like 'pinching' the neck between your thumb and forefinger. Fretting will be explained in more detail later on in the book.

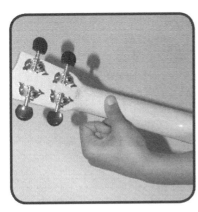

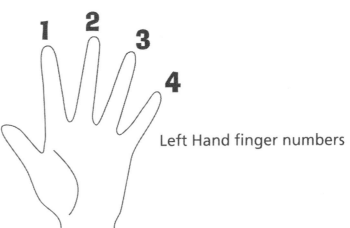

Left Hand finger numbers

RIGHT HAND POSITION

Because the ukulele is such a light instrument you can hold it between your right forearm and your body. Hold it in place by pushing it gently against the bottom of your ribcage. This works for both a seated and a standing playing position. You can then strum from the wrist so your forearm can keep the ukulele close to your body.

Left Handed Players

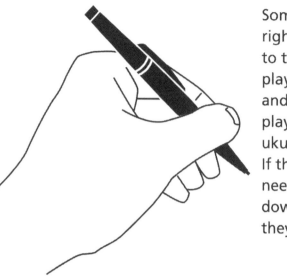

Some left handed players play the ukulele right-handed (with the headstock pointing to the left). If you are left-handed try the playing in the right hand position shown and see how it feels. If it feels strange, try playing it the other way round (with the ukulele headstock pointing to your right). If this feels more comfortable then you'll need to have the ukulele re-strung upside down. Ask at your local music store — they should be able to do this for you.

Using A Plectrum / Pick

You can use your right hand fingers to play a ukulele but many players use a plectrum (often called a pick) to strum chords. Strum across the strings where the neck joins the body of the ukulele. This produces a bright sound. If strumming with your fingers (without a pick) use your thumb to strum downwards and your index finger for the upstroke.

Picks come in different thicknesses. A medium pick is probably the best one to start with.

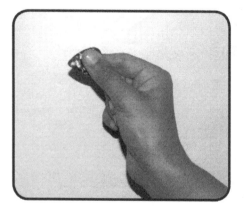

Tuning

The strings of the ukulele are tuned to the notes **G**, **C**, **E** and **A**. These strings are known as the 'open' strings. Pressing down on a string with a left hand finger to change the pitch of the note is called **fretting**.

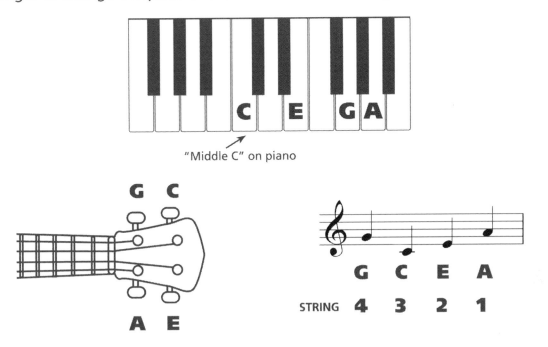

"Middle C" on piano

To keep your ukulele in tune you can use a piano to help you find the notes or you can use one of the many digital tuning 'apps' now available for smartphones and laptops. There are also certain websites which give you a 'player' which allows you to play the notes and tune your uke.

TUNING PEGS	To Make Your Note Lower	To Make Your Note Higher
TURN PEGS ON TOP ROW (**G** & **C** strings)	CLOCKWISE	ANTI-CLOCKWISE
TURN PEGS ON BOTTOM ROW (**E** & **A** strings)	ANTI-CLOCKWISE	CLOCKWISE

* You may like to ask an adult to help you tune your uke before you begin.

Chords And Strumming

Chords are made up of two or more notes played together at the same time. Earlier we told you about your right hand and holding a pick and now we'll show you how strumming works.

To start with we'll just use the open strings to practice this. This means you don't have to push any strings down with your left hand fingers. You may need to hold the neck of your ukulele to keep it steady whilst you do this.

First of all bring your right hand up above the strings holding your thumb (or pick) out.

Then bring your hand down and use your thumb (or pick) to stroke across the strings.

Follow the strum through until you've played across all four strings.

STRUM!

Well done! You have just strummed a DOWNSTROKE!

How To Read Chord Diagrams

Now we'll try playing chords, which means using our left hand as well as our right. To do this you will need to fret the notes of the chord. This means you'll use the fingers of your left hand to push down on one or more string.

Chords are played using 'shapes' which are written using chord diagrams. Chord diagrams are simple box diagrams for each chord, showing you where to put your left hand fingers on the frets.

The fingerings are marked just above each box in line with the string below them.

If the fingering reads '0' then allow that particular string to ring 'open' — you don't use any left hand fingers to fret on that string. If it reads say, 2, it means you use your 2nd **finger** to push down on the fret shown — the black dot shows us where.

REMINDER!

STRINGS

④ ③ ② ①

1
2 FRETS
3
4

Example: C Chord

LEFT HAND
FINGER NUMBERS   0   0   0   3

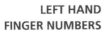

PUSH DOWN
ON THE 3RD FRET
OF THIS STRING

LEFT HAND
FINGER NUMBERS

1   2   3
4

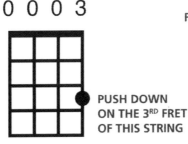

So, for the **C** chord we need to use our 3rd **finger** on our left hand, to push down on the 3rd **fret** on the top (**A**) string.

*Be sure to push your finger down on the string **JUST ABOVE** the metal fret, not on top of it!*

The Chord Of C

This is nice and easy because you only need to push down with one left hand finger. Position your left hand thumb behind the neck as shown on page 7, and push down on your **A** string with your **3rd finger** on the **3rd fret**.

Limericks and rhymes are always a fun way to practice your chords and make people laugh at the same time!

Strum a downstroke on your **C** chord whenever you see a word in **BOLD**. The chord name will be written above to remind you.

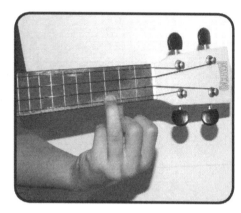

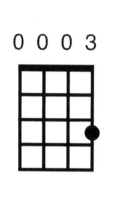

   C   **C**
I **love** that I'm playing the **uke**

    C   **C**
And **learning** so much from this **book**

    C
It's **easy** and fun

    C
And I've **only** begun

   C   **C**
In **no** time at all that it **took**!

The Chord Of F

Time to learn a new chord!

Let's do **F** next.

You will need two fingers to push down for this one.

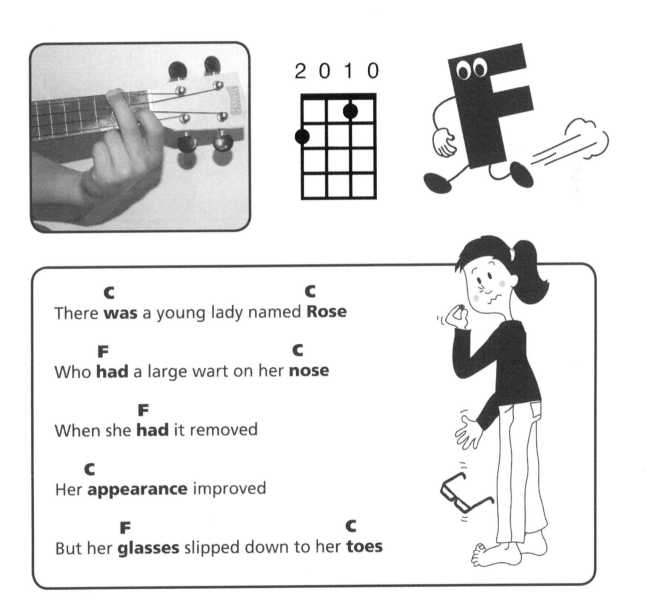

2 0 1 0

```
        C                    C
There was a young lady named Rose

        F                 C
Who had a large wart on her nose

            F
When she had it removed

    C
Her appearance improved

        F                      C
But her glasses slipped down to her toes
```

The Chord Of G7

Now let's learn our third chord — **G7**.

0 2 1 3

This last limerick has all three chords in. Take it slowly at first until you get used to the changes between chords

    C   **C**
There **was** an Old Man in a **tree**

    F   **C**
Who was **horribly** bugged by a **bee**;

    F
When they **said**, "Does it buzz?"

    C
He re-**plied**, "Yes, it does!"

    G7   **C**
"And it's **currently** stinging my **knee**"

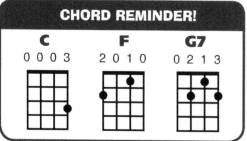

CHORD REMINDER!

C	F	G7
0 0 0 3	2 0 1 0	0 2 1 3

The Chord Of A Minor

Try playing your new **A minor chord** below — it's written down as **Am** — the little **m** stands for **minor**! Have a listen to the chord, some people think minor chords sound sad...what do you think?

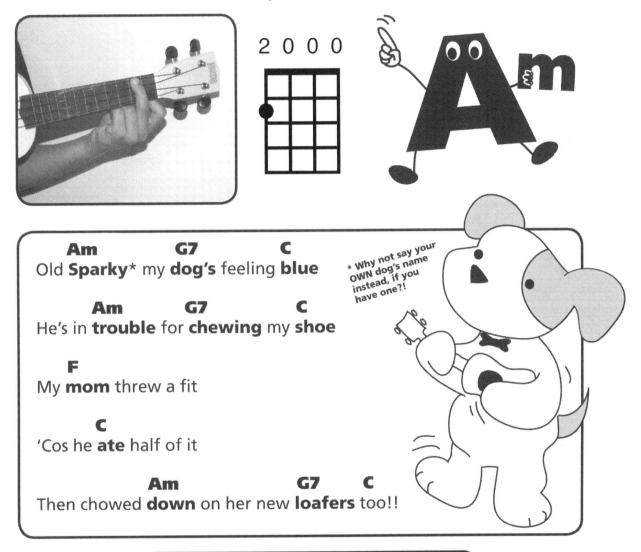

2 0 0 0

Am   **G7**   **C**
Old **Sparky*** my **dog's** feeling **blue**

Am   **G7**   **C**
He's in **trouble** for **chewing** my **shoe**

F
My **mom** threw a fit

C
'Cos he **ate** half of it

Am   **G7**   **C**
Then chowed **down** on her new **loafers** too!!

* Why not say your OWN dog's name instead, if you have one?!

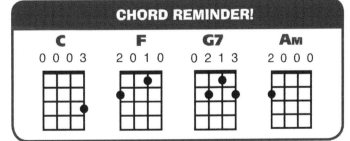

CHORD REMINDER!

C	F	G7	Am
0 0 0 3	2 0 1 0	0 2 1 3	2 0 0 0

# Strumming Patterns

When you use a mixture of down strokes and up strokes it is called a strumming pattern. Let's try a simple one first:

Hold down a **C** chord and try playing 4 down strokes as shown below.

Count 1, 2, 3, 4 as you strum *downwards*.

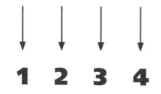

Now try an *upstroke*. Use the index or 1st finger of your right hand (or pick if you use one) for this and brush upwards across the strings.

Now try going between the *down-stroke* and the *up-stroke*. Still counting but saying '*and*' on the upstroke at the end of the pattern.

Now try an *upstroke after* every *downstroke*:

1 *and* **2** *and* **3** *and* **4** *and*

You're now ready to try playing through a proper song. This first verse of 'Wheels On The Bus' is written in musical form using bars (or measures).

First let's try a simple strumming pattern, using only a **DOWN** stroke and just 2 chords — **C** and **G7**.

CHORD REMINDER!

C   G7
0 0 0 3   0 2 1 3

The Wheels On The Bus

C
The wheels on the bus go round and round,

G⁷
round and round, round and round the

C
wheels on the bus go round and round

G⁷   C
all   through   the town

Now let's try the song again, using **DOWN and UP** strokes.

Notice how the strokes are played as you sing a particular word of the song. Sometimes you will use a down stroke quickly followed by and up stroke. Let's call this the **'DOWN/UP'** stroke.

The Wheels On The Bus

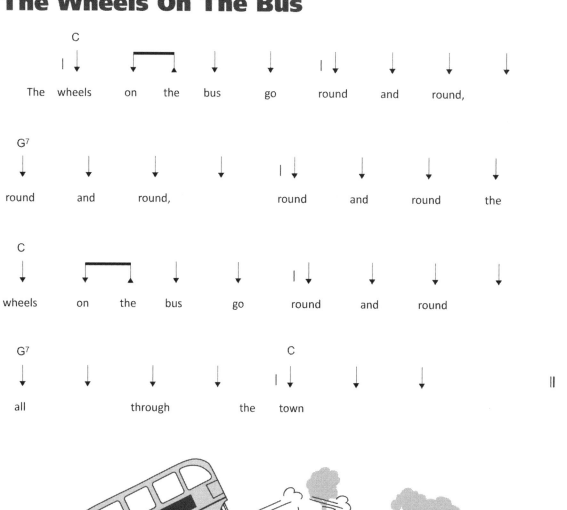

G7   C

all   through   the   town

Now you can play the rest of the song using exactly the same strumming pattern. Here are the rest of the words. Don't forget to use your *DOWN/UP* stroke each time you sing '*on the*', and change chords where indicated:

2
C
The wipers *on the* bus go
Swish, swish, swish

G7
Swish, swish, swish
Swish, swish, swish

C
The wipers *on the* bus go
Swish, swish, swish

G7   **C**
All through the town

3
C
The horn *on the* bus goes
Beep, beep, beep

G7
Beep, beep, beep
Beep, beep, beep

C
The horn *on the* bus goes
Beep, beep, beep

G7   **C**
All through the town

4
C
The money *on the* bus goes
Clink, clink, clink

G7
Clink, clink, clink,
Clink, clink, clink.

C
The money *on the* bus goes,
Clink, clink, clink

G7   **C**
All through the town

5
C
The driver *on the* bus says
"Move on back

G7
move on back
move on back"

C
The driver *on the* bus says
"Move on back"

G7   **C**
All through the town

6
C
The people *on the* bus go
Up and down

G7
Up and down
Up and down

C
The people *on the* bus go
Up and down

G7   **C**
All through the town

7
C
The baby *on the* bus says
"Wah, wah, wah

G7
Wah, wah, wah
Wah, wah, wah"

C
The baby *on the* bus says
"Wah, wah, wah"

G7   **C**
All through the town

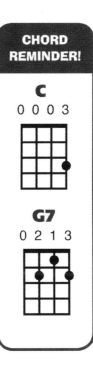

CHORD REMINDER!

C
0 0 0 3

G7
0 2 1 3

If You're Happy And You Know It

Now let's try a new song, using the same chords — **C** and **G7**.

2
C
If you're happy and you know it

G7
Stomp your feet (stomp stomp)

If you're happy and you know it

C
Stomp your feet (stomp stomp)

F
If you're happy and you know it

C
And you really want to show it

G7
If you're happy and you know it

C
Stomp your feet (stomp stomp)

3
C
If you're happy and you know it

G7
Shout "Hurray!" (hoo-ray!)

If you're happy and you know it

C
Shout "Hurray!" (hoo-ray!)

F
If you're happy and you know it

C
And you really want to show it

G7
If you're happy and you know it

C
Shout "Hurray!" (hoo-ray!)

4
C
If you're happy and you know it

G7
Do all three
(clap-clap, stomp-stomp, hoo-ray!)

If you're happy and you know it

C
Do all three
(clap-clap, stomp-stomp, hoo-ray!)

F
If you're happy and you know it

C
And you really want to show it

G7
If you're happy and you know it

C
Do all three

Hooray!!

Old Macdonald Had A Farm

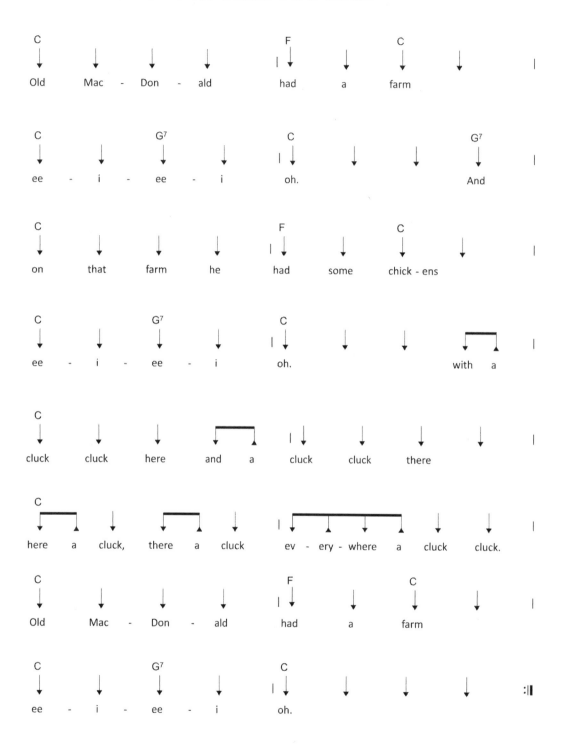

2 C   F   C   G7 C
Old MacDonald had a farm, ee i ee i oh

C   F   C   G7 C
And on that farm he had some dogs, ee i ee i oh
With a woof-woof here and a woof-woof there

Here a woof, there a woof, everywhere a woof-woof

      F   C   G7 C
Old MacDonald had a farm, ee i ee i oh

3 C   F   C   G7 C
Old MacDonald had a farm, ee i ee i oh

C   F   C   G7 C
And on that farm he had some turkeys, ee i ee i oh

With a woof-woof here and a woof-woof there

Here a woof, there a cluck, everywhere a cluck-cluck

      F   C   G7 C
Old MacDonald had a farm, ee i ee i oh

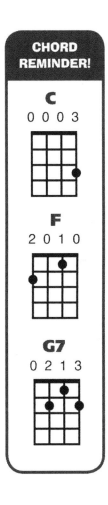

4 C   F   C   G7 C
Old MacDonald had a farm, ee i ee i oh

       F   C   G7 C
And on that farm he had some turkeys, ee i ee i oh

With a gobble-gobble here and a gobble-gobble there

Here a gobble, there a gobble, everywhere a gobble-gobble

      F   C   G7 C
Old MacDonald had a farm, ee i ee i oh

Baa Baa Black Sheep

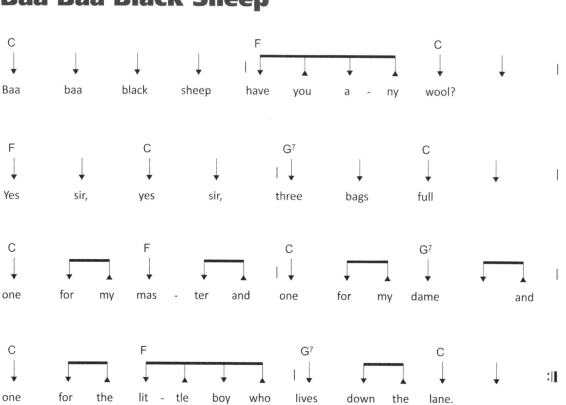

Hickory Dickory Dock

C	G7	C			C	G7	C			
Hickory	dickory	dock			the mouse ran	up	the clock.		The	

C	G7	F	C		G7		C			
clock struck	one the	mouse	ran down		hickory		dickory	dock		:‖

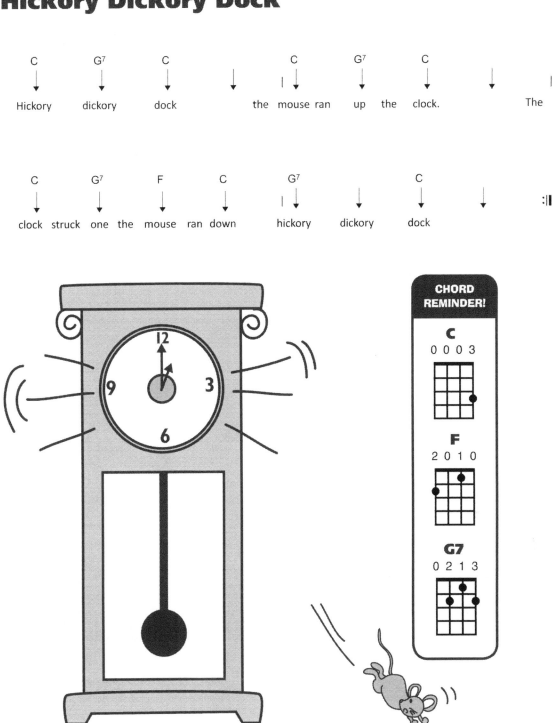

CHORD REMINDER!

C
0 0 0 3

F
2 0 1 0

G7
0 2 1 3

Yankee Doodle

C									C				G⁷	
Yank	- ee	doo	- dle	went	to	town	a		ri	- ding	on	a	po	- ny

C				F				G⁷				C	
stuck	a	fea	- ther	in	his	cap	and	called	it	mac	- a	- ro	- ni

F							C					
Yank	- ee	doo	- dle	keep	it	up	Yank	- ee	doo	- dle	dan	- dy

F							C		G⁷		C	
mind	the	mu	- sic	and	the	step	and	with	the	girls	be	han	- dy

CHORD REMINDER!

C	F	G7
0 0 0 3	2 0 1 0	0 2 1 3

Twinkle Twinkle Little Star

C			F	C	
Twin - kle,	twin - kle,	lit - tle	star		

F	C	G⁷	C	
how I	won - der	what you	are	

C	F	C	G⁷	
Up a - bove	the word	so	high	

C	F	C	G⁷	
like a	dia - mond in	the	sky	

CHORD REMINDER!

C	F	G7
0 0 0 3	2 0 1 0	0 2 1 3

Oh Little Town Of Bethlehem

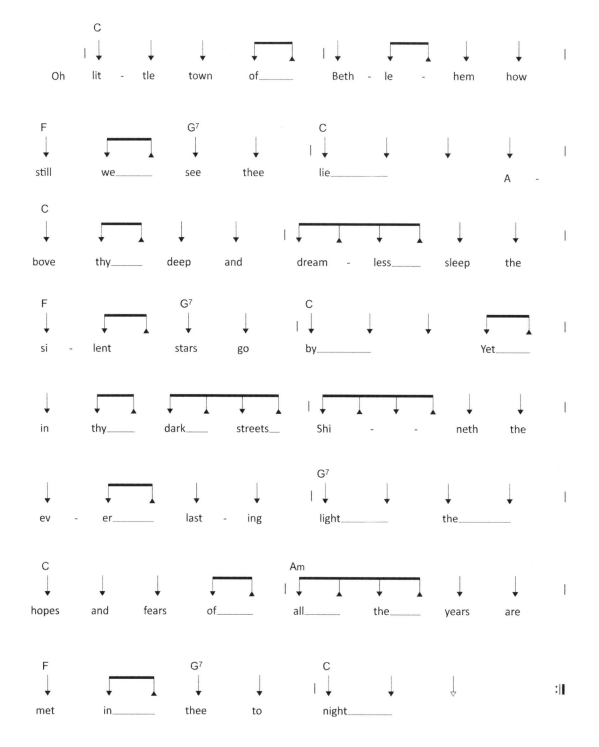

C

Oh lit - tle town of_____ Beth - le - hem how

F   G⁷   C

still we_____ see thee lie_____ A -

C

bove thy_____ deep and dream - less_____ sleep the

F   G⁷   C

si - lent stars go by_____ Yet_____

in thy_____ dark_____ streets_____ Shi - - neth the

G⁷

ev - er_____ last - ing light_____ the_____

C   Am

hopes and fears of_____ all_____ the_____ years are

F   G⁷   C

met in_____ thee to night_____

2

C
O morning stars, together

    F   G7   C
Proclaim the holy birth!

And praises sing to God the King

    F   G7   C
And peace to men on earth

For Christ is born of Mary

       G7
And gathered all above

   C   Am
While mortals sleep the Angels keep

    F   G7   C
Their watch of wondering love

3

C
How silently, how silently

    F   G7   C
The wondrous gift is given

   C
So God imparts to human hearts

    F   G7   C
The blessings of His Heaven

No ear may hear His coming

        G7
But in this world of sin

   C   Am
Where meek souls will receive Him still

F   G7   C
The dear Christ enters in

4

C
O holy Child of Bethlehem

    F   G7   C
Descend to us, we pray!

Cast out our sin and enter in

    F   G7   C
Be born in us to-day

We hear the Christmas angels

          G7
The great glad tidings tell

   C   Am
O come to us, abide with us

    F   G7   C
Our Lord Em-man-uel!

CHORD REMINDER!

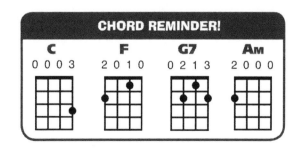

C	F	G7	Am
0 0 0 3	2 0 1 0	0 2 1 3	2 0 0 0

Quiz: Name Parts of the Ukulele

Fretboard

Headstock

Tuning Pegs

Bridge

Body

Strings

Nut

Frets

Soundhole

Neck

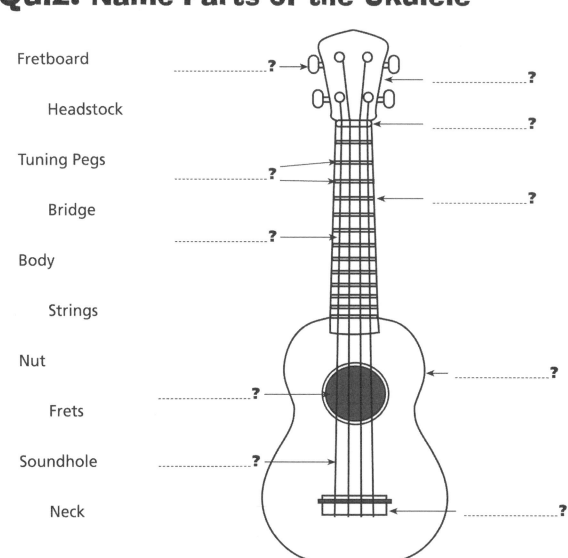

Quiz: Name That Chord

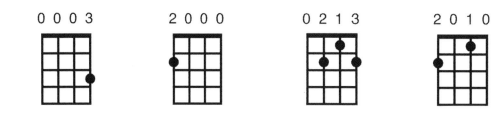

0 0 0 3   2 0 0 0   0 2 1 3   2 0 1 0

MORE GREAT MUSIC BOOKS FROM KYLE CRAIG!

How To Play UKULELE — A Complete Guide for Absolute Beginners

978-1-908-707-08-6

My First UKULELE — Learn to Play: Kids

978-1-908-707-11-6

Easy UKULELE Tunes

978-1-908707-37-6

How To Play GUITAR — A Complete Guide for Absolute Beginners

978-1-908-707-09-3

My First GUITAR — Learn to Play: Kids

978-1-908-707-13-0

Easy GUITAR Tunes

978-1-908707-34-5

How To Play KEYBOARD — A Complete Guide for Absolute Beginners

978-1-908-707-14-7

My First KEYBOARD — Learn to Play: Kids

978-1-908-707-15-4

Easy KEYBOARD Tunes

978-1-908707-35-2

How To Play PIANO — A Complete Guide for Absolute Beginners

978-1-908-707-16-1

My First PIANO — Learn to Play: Kids

978-1-908-707-17-8

Easy PIANO Tunes

978-1-908707-33-8

How To Play HARMONICA — A Complete Guide for Absolute Beginners

978-1-908-707-28-4

My First RECORDER — Learn to Play: Kids

978-1-908-707-18-5

Easy RECORDER Tunes

978-1-908707-36-9

How To Play BANJO — A Complete Guide for Absolute Beginners

978-1-908-707-19-2

The GUITAR Chord Dictionary

978-1-908707-39-0

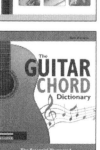

The UKULELE Chord Dictionary

978-1-908707-38-3

Made in the USA
San Bernardino, CA
31 May 2018